W9-AZC-778

THE CAT'S MEOW

Feline Answers to Life's **BIG** Questions

BILL ZIMMERMAN
ILLUSTRATED BY TOM BLOOM

WILLOW CREEK PRESS
Minocqua, Wisconsin

Published by Willow Creek Press

P.O. Box 147, Minocqua, Wisconsin 54548

www.willowcreekpress.com

Editor: Andrea Donner

Design: Katrin Wooley

Originally published as *Cat-e-Chisms: Feline Answers to Life's Big Questions* in 1997 by Hazelden.

Library of Congress Cataloging-in-Publication Data

Zimmerman, William, 1941-

  The cat's meow : feline ansers to life's big questions / Bill Zimmerman ; illustrations by Tom Bloom.

      p.cm.

  ISBN 1-57223-585-8 (hardcover : alk. paper)

  1. Cats--Humor. 2. Conduct of life--Humor. 3. Cats--Caricatures and cartoons. 4. Cats--Pictorial works. I. Title.

PN6231.C23Z58 2003

818'.5402--dc21

                                                2003002525

Printed in Canada

*In memory of my dear, sweet, gentle friend,
Arthur Hamparian.*

*And to my daughter, Carlota, who opens her heart
to God's little creatures.*
—B.Z.

PURR-WORD

How many of us wake up in the morning asking ourselves, "What is the meaning of our lives?" Sometimes the answer is right before our eyes, on top of or under the bed, in the form of four-footed creatures, the cat, who waits impatiently for us to wake up, pet it, and feed it.

Maybe the meaning of our lives is found in the way we show our love for others, including our friend the cat. The unselfish way in which we care for, soothe, and nurture these little beings manifests the constancy of our love. This caring also provides us with a center around which we can construct our lives.

When spending time with your cat, if you watch carefully and listen intently, you will discover some answers to the big questions of life that are raised in this book: What are life's basic rules? How do we make the most of our days and lead meaningful lives? What are the pleasures of life?

Your cat knows these answers—yes, indeed—so listen carefully as it purrs its comfort and mystery to you, and don't worry if your cat resides solely in your imagination.

Bill Zimmerman

LIFE

FIRST **BIG** QUESTION

WHAT ARE LIFE'S BASIC RULES?

ALWAYS RETAIN A LITTLE
WILDNESS IN YOU.

BEING UNPREDICTABLE IS, AFTER ALL,
WHAT MAKES YOU SO EXCITING.

CALL THE SHOTS IN YOUR GAME.
LET OTHERS HUG YOU
ONLY WHEN YOU
FEEL LIKE IT.

DON'T ALLOW YOURSELF TO BE
EASILY TAKEN OVER.

© Diane Ensign

8

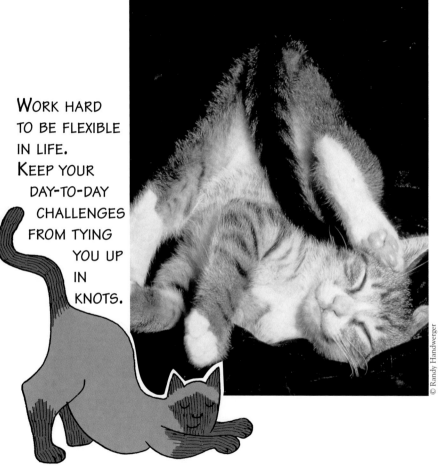

WORK HARD
TO BE FLEXIBLE
IN LIFE.
KEEP YOUR
DAY-TO-DAY
CHALLENGES
FROM TYING
YOU UP
IN
KNOTS.

© Randy Handwerger

9

Dear Tabby,
   Life has lost its zest for me. Even catnip
                         thrills me no more.
                              What should I do?
                                   Bored
                                   Siamese

Dear Bored,
You must challenge yourself to scale new heights in life periodically. Set new goals daily; don't be content with the ordinary... it'll wear you down, and make you dog-tired.
                         Sincerely, Tabby

TAKE A CATNAP WHENEVER
YOU SEE A WINDOW OF
OPPORTUNITY.
OR JUST A WINDOW.
YOU'LL NEED SOME REST
FOR NEW ADVENTURES.

11

WAIT AND WATCH.

THE CAT'S MEOW

LIFE WILL REVEAL ITS SECRETS TO YOU.

MEW SING

KEEP AN EYE ON THE CANARIES.

© George Harrison

12

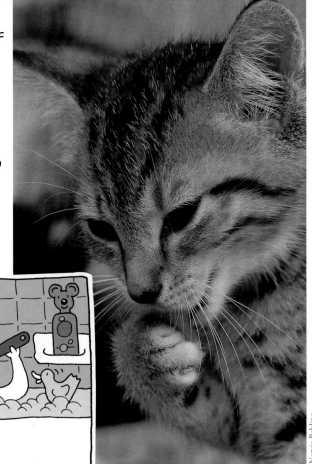

KEEP YOURSELF CLEAN AND READY TO BE ADMIRED. REMEMBER TO LICK YOUR WHISKERS AND WASH BEHIND YOUR EARS. MAKE IT A RITUAL.

SOMETIMES YOU NEED
TO CLING TO OTHERS.

© Alan & Sandy Carey

SOMETIMES YOU'VE JUST GOT TO LET GO.

LOOK UPON THE WORLD AS YOUR CATNIP TOY. ENJOY IT FULLY.

© RonKimballStock.com

PURR FROM DEEP WITHIN YOUR SOUL.

ALWAYS TRY TO
LAND ON
YOUR FEET...
NOT ON
YOUR HEAD.

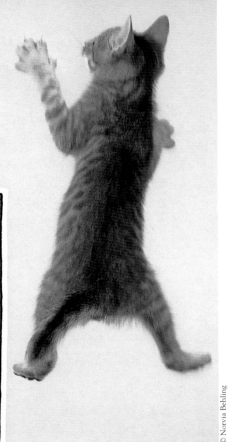

Dear Tabby,
My true love has a pedigree, while I come from much more humble origins. Is there a future for us?

Unsure
Short Hair

Dear Unsure,
Pedigree is not the end-all, be-all; what does count in life is how well we lead our lives and how we treat others. How you project yourself will be how others perceive you, be it purebred or alley cat. Remember, within each of us there resides an aristocat. Respect yourself.
Yours, Tabby

LEARN HOW TO KEEP A SECRET.

DON'T SPILL ALL THE BEANS, THE WAY A DOG WOULD.

© Norvia Behling

19

THE
CAT'S
MEOW

KEEP YOUR
OWN
COUNSEL.
TRUST YOUR
JUDGMENT.

MEW
SING

BECOME PART OF THE SILENCE THAT YOU WATCH.

© Terry Wild Studio

20

WHILE THINGS MAY CHANGE AROUND YOU, STAY CENTERED ON THE CORE OF YOUR BEING.

THAT WILL GET YOU THROUGH TUMULTUOUS TIMES.

Never, ever lose your sense of curiosity (despite what you've heard).

© Bonnie Nance

That is the way you learn and remain kitten-like.

Dear Tabby,
There are times when I cannot make a decision. I wander about and question everything but just can't make up my mind. How can I correct this?
Confused Persian

Dear Confused,
Trust your senses (including your sixth one... whatever it is); they will always lead you through life's wandering paths. And don't forget to use your ears and even your whiskers to pick up guiding vibrations in the air.

Truly, Tabby

24

WATCH AND SNIFF AND LISTEN.

BE ALERT TO THE SIGNS AROUND YOU
AND THE MOODS OF OTHERS.

EXPLORE THE OUTSIDE
WORLD ALL YOU WANT,

BUT REMEMBER WHEN
TO COME HOME.

© Randy Handwerger

CLIMB TO THE
HIGHEST HEIGHT
THAT YOU CAN
ACHIEVE.

BUT BE CAUTIOUS.
DON'T GO OUT
ON A LIMB FOR
LOST CAUSES.

© Sharon Eide / Elizabeth Flynn

GIVE YOURSELF TIME. SPACE. RESPECT.

THE CAT'S MEOW

© Frank S. Balthis

MEW SING

SEEK OUT HIDDEN, SECRET CORNERS.

BE CALM AND PATIENT.

LET YOUR SELF-POSSESSION SET A GOOD EXAMPLE FOR OTHERS.

31

Dear Tabby,
Sometimes I think my humans take me for granted. They don't seem to accord me the proper respect, even though I purr and nuzzle them whenever I can. Is it me, or is it them?
Humbled Russian Blue

Dear Humbled,
Are you catatonic? You seem to have forgotten that cardinal rule... be mysterious! Convey that you have a secret life and humans will beg to enter it. However, you do not necessarily have to let them in. Simply put, learn to be a bit more independent.
Yours in shock, Tabby

CHOOSE A ROLE FOR
YOURSELF IN LIFE...
WILL YOU BE A...
TOP CAT? FAT CAT? SCAREDY
CAT? SMART CAT? HEP CAT?
SCAT CAT? COOL CAT?
PUSSY CAT OR TOM CAT?
WHAT'S IT GOING TO BE?

IF YOU'RE NOT
SURE, WHY NOT TRY
THEM ALL ON TO SEE WHICH ONE FITS BEST?
YOU CAN RE-INVENT YOUR LIFE WHENEVER YOU WISH.

THERE IS A TIME
TO BE KITTENISH...
AND A TIME TO BE
SLY AND CUNNING.

LIFE IS NOT JUST
ONE THING.

© Bonnie Nance

EVERY ONE OF US,

INCLUDING **YOU**

NEEDS TO BE SOMEONE'S BOON
COMPANION AS WELL AS
THE AFFECTIONATE RECIPIENT
OF HUMAN KINDNESS.

© Bonnie Nance

You're on the air with Emily Scratching Post...
...YEAH, SO HERE'S MY QUESTION... TO BE INDEPENDENT OR NOT TO BE? TO RUN LOOSE EACH DAY AND NIGHT, OR STAY HOME WHERE IT'S COZY AND WARM? WHICH PATH IS THE RIGHT ONE?
...Yes, yes.... ...always try to be as independent as possible. Remember, there are times when we NEED a lap on which to lay our head. But, you can carry this independence thing too far, too. Full freedom, while exhilarating, can be lonely, too. Thank you for calling...
1 2 3
CAT CHAT

FILL UP A ROOM WITH YOUR PRESENCE.

© Diane Ensign

SURVEY YOUR DOMAIN AND DECIDE WHAT SPOT(S) SUIT(S) YOU BEST.

THE CAT'S MEOW

MAKE SOMEONE YOU KNOW PURR TODAY.

© Alan & Sandy Carey

MEW SING

WAIT EAGERLY FOR THE NIGHT. MAKE PLANS.

41

WHEN YOU SEE SOMETHING YOU REALLY WANT, RUN!
LEAP! POUNCE ON IT WITH ALL OF YOUR PASSION!

© Reed/Williams / AnimalsAnimals

DON'T GO
HUNTING HALF-HEARTEDLY AFTER YOUR QUEST.

CAT TALES ... Paws to Refresh

© Alan & Sandy Carey

ANYTHING CAN BE A TOY,
ANY MOMENT AN OCCASION
TO PLAY,

SO GIVE IN TO YOUR
HIGH SPIRITS
AND JOY OF LIFE.

© Alan & Sandy Carey

44

WITH WILL AND DETERMINATION YOU CAN NAVIGATE TIGHT
SPACES AND EXPLORE HIDDEN LANDS THAT
OTHERS MAY HAVE DEEMED INACCESSIBLE.

© Norvia Behling

JUST BE FLEXIBLE
IN YOUR APPROACH.

45

You're on the air with Emily Scratching Post...

YOU KNOW, SOMETIMES I FEAR THAT LIFE IS PASSING ME BY. I FEEL I SHOULD BE DOING THINGS ALL THE TIME, BUT TO TELL THE TRUTH, I AM JUST TOO TIRED. WHAT WOULD YOUR ADVICE BE?

Well, you've got my go-ahead to take some time off now and then to watch the sunlight travel across a room, stare at people. That's fun! Chase a butterfly one day, some fireflies that night. Gaze at the stars. Enjoy, and you'll soon feel rejuvenated.
Good luck to you!

47

BE WATCHFUL.

YOU CAN LEARN A LOT FROM THE SMALLEST INSECT OR FROM THE PLAY BETWEEN SHADOW AND LIGHT. THESE ARE TINY MIRACLES.

© Norvia Behling

DON'T JUST GIVE AWAY YOUR LOVE; REMEMBER, YOU ARE NOT THE DOG.

THE CAT'S MEOW

MEW SING

WATCH THE WORLD FROM A WARM WINDOWSILL.

IF YOU DON'T LIKE SOMETHING, IT'S OK
TO EXPRESS YOUR DISPLEASURE;

A CATCALL WILL DO NICELY,
THANK YOU.

IT IS WISE TO KNOW WHEN TO PLEASE OTHERS, TO MAKE THEM HAPPY.

PURR, RUB BACK AND FORTH, GIVE SOMEONE A SMALL LICK; LIFE CANNOT ALWAYS BE LIVED ON YOUR TERMS.

PROVIDE TRANQUILITY FOR OTHERS WITH YOUR COMFORTING PRESENCE.

DON'T HESITATE TO HELP THEM IN THEIR TIME OF NEED.

© Bonnie Nance

53

© Norvia Behling

55

DON'T BE AFRAID OF THE DARKNESS. LET YOUR EYES SHINE INTO THE NIGHT.

THERE IS MUCH TO BE GAINED FROM STEALTH AND SILENCE.

FIND YOUR PLACE IN THE SCHEME OF THINGS.

POSITION YOURSELF CAREFULLY. THEN TAKE A LITTLE NAP. IT'LL STILL BE THERE WHEN YOU AWAKE.

© RonKimballStock.com

58

LOVE, NURTURE, AND CARE

FOR THE KITTIES THAT YOU BRING INTO THIS WORLD.

YOUR DEVOTION WILL ENABLE THEM TO BECOME COMPETENT INDIVIDUALS.

THE CAT'S MEOW

TRY TO MAINTAIN AN INTIMATE RELATIONSHIP
WITH THE WORLD.

MEW SING

JUMP FARTHER THAN YOU DID YESTERDAY.

You're on the air with Emily Scratching Post...

...I'M HIGHSTRUNG AND KINDA SKITTISH BY NATURE, AND, UM, WELL, EVERYTHING SEEMS TO GET TO ME. IT'S, UH, IT'S DIFFICULT FOR ME TO SLOW DOWN, PACE MYSELF, SEE? I MEAN THERE'S JUST NOT ENOUGH TIME, YOU KNOW? SO, SO, SO, WHAT CAN I DO?

...Well, first, RELAX and take a slow, deep breath. Edginess can be a useful way to stay attuned to the world, but it can also put you OVER the edge. Here's what to do, find a quiet corner and try to settle down. You need to create a balance in your life. It's like chasing a mouse or catching a mouse. It's a mad dash that's fun to do. I know you can, you must.

63

THERE'S A TIME
TO MEW SOFTLY
AND
SWEETLY,

AND A TIME TO
GROWL AND
HISSSSS.

DO EACH WITH DISCRETION.

>> A CAT SIGH <<

SOMETIMES IT'S NICE JUST TO SIT BY THE WINDOW AND WATCH THE WORLD GO BY.

© Alan & Sandy Carey

DOMINATE YOUR ENVIRONMENT

© Bonnie Nance

ALWAYS
PLAY AND FROLIC.
NO CALLING IS MORE
NOBLE. ROMP, ROLL,
AND TUMBLE. LIFE IS
SHORT. (EVEN IF YOU
HAVE NINE.)

68

FIND OUT WHAT YOUR CATNIP IN LIFE IS. LET ITS JOY HIT YOU WITH FULL FORCE.

EATING IS SUCH A DELIGHT, MADE MORE SO BY NIBBLING FROM THE DISH OF A LOVED ONE.

THE CAT'S MEOW

MEW SING

STRETCH, S T R E T C H, STRETCH.

ENGAGE IN
THE CHASE.

© RonKimballStock.com

YOU DON'T HAVE
TO WIN...
JUST ENJOY
THE GAME.

KNOW
WHEN TO BE...

☐ RESERVED,
☐ INQUISITIVE,
☐ FLIRTATIOUS,
☐ INDIFFERENT,
☐ CONTEMPLATIVE,
☐ INDEPENDENT,
☐ JUBILANT,
☐ CAUTIOUS,
☐ PRACTICAL.

>> A CAT SIGH

© SparrasPhoto.com

CLIMB UP THE DRAPES. ENJOY THE VIEW.

MEW SING

73

© Sharon Eide / Elizabeth Flynn

75

JUST AS YOU ACCEPT YOUR CAT'S IDIOSYNCRASIES, LEARN, TOO, TO ACCEPT THEM IN YOURSELF AND OTHERS.

NOT EVERYONE HAS TO BE THE SAME.

© RonKimballStock.com

SURRENDER TO THE SUN.
LET ITS WARMTH SOOTHE
YOU AS YOU SNOOZE
IN ITS RESTFUL RAYS.

77

THE CAT'S MEOW

TAKE PLEASURE IN THE DAILY ROUTINES OF LIFE.

MEW SING

KISS THE KITTIES. OFTEN. HUG THEM, TOO.

© Alan & Sandy Carey

78

LET YOURSELF
BE CUDDLED
IN SOMEONE'S
ARMS.

EACH OF US
NEEDS A PLACE
OF COMFORT
FROM TIME TO
TIME. WHY
SHOULD YOU BE
DIFFERENT?

© Karen Hudson

WHEN YOU ARE
ALERT AND HAPPY,
EXHIBIT YOUR
FEELINGS OF

WELL-
BEING TO
OTHERS.

BE KIND AND
PURR A
LITTLE
>>THANK YOU.<<

DON'T HOLD A GRUDGE. AT SOME POINT IT'S BEST TO MAKE PEACE WITH YOUR ENEMIES.

© Norvia Behling

YOU SHOULDN'T SPEND YOUR PRECIOUS LIFE FIGHTING.

THE CAT'S MEOW

CULTIVATE YOUR
NATURAL SKILLS
OF DEXTERITY
AND INGENUITY.
THEY WILL HELP
LEAD YOU TO
SAFETY.

INTERRUPT THE PATH OF A BUG.

MEW SING

SCHEDULE LOTS OF **R&R** INTO YOUR DAILY ROUTINE.

BUT YOU KNOW THIS ALREADY!

© Bonnie Nance

83

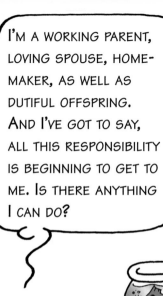

84

85

FIND A FENCE TO SIT ON AND GAZE WITH WONDER AT THE MOON.

BUT TRY NOT TO WAKE THE NEIGHBORS.

© Rolf Kopfle

86

BE WISE.

RELAX.

ALLOW SOMEONE TO PET YOU TODAY.

© Bonnie Nance

87

WELCOME THE NIGHT. LET THE DARK BE YOUR COVER.

EXPLORE OUR WONDERFUL WORLD.

IT CAN BE A GREAT TIME OF DISCOVERY AND FUN FOR YOU.

© Alan & Sandy Carey

CAT TALES ... Claws & Effect

© Frank S. Balthis

89

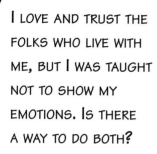

90

WHEN THE MOMENT HITS YOU,

© Robert Maier / AnimalsAnimals

GIVE IN TO THE SIREN SONG
OF LOVE.

TAKE COMFORT IN THE MYSTICAL SIDE OF YOUR NATURE.

LISTEN FOR THE SECRETS OF THE UNIVERSE.

GAZE INTO THE UNKNOWN.

BILL ZIMMERMAN, the creator of The Cat's Meow, *has been a questioner all his life. A journalist for more than twenty years and a prize-winning editor, Zimmerman is special projects editor for* Newsday, *one of the nation's largest newspapers. His other books are* The Dog's Bark: Simple Truths from a Wise Pet; The Little Book of Joy: An Interactive Journal for Thoughts, Prayers, and Wishes; How to Tape Instant Oral Biographies, *a book that teaches readers how to capture family stories on audio- and video-tape;* Make Beliefs, *a magical gift book for the imagination;* Lifelines: A Book of Hope, *which offers comforting thoughts;* A Book of Questions to Keep Thoughts and Feelings, *a new form of diary/journal;* Make Beliefs for Kids of All Ages; *and* A Book of Sunshine, *to move clouds in your life. Zimmerman also runs Guarionex Press, which develops and publishes books that affirm the power of imagination and human spirit to overcome life's problems.*

TOM BLOOM has had four cats thus far, cohabitating with as many as three at once. However, at no time has he ever thought of himself as a feline, as it would be too difficult for furry little paws to draw funny little pictures for the New York Times, Newsday, Forbes, Barron's, Fortune, *and* Games Magazine. *Bloom and his family are currently living a catless existence in a remarkably mouse-free house. He is also very fond of the occasional catnap.*

SHARE WITH US

Dear Reader,
Please share with us the simple truths you have learned from your own pet. Perhaps we can incorporate some of them in future editions. We also welcome your comments and suggestions to make The Cat's Meow *funnier and wiser. Please write to: Bill Zimmerman, Guarionex Press, 201 West 77th Street, New York, NY 10024.*

A CAT SIGH

REMEMBER-- SNEAK AWAY FOR SOME TOMFOOLERY WHEN THINGS GET TO BE TOO MUCH FOR YOU.

GET INTO A LITTLE MISCHIEF.